EASTER VIGIL HOMILIES

Easter Vigil Homilies

Jorge Mario Bergoglio/
Pope Francis

LITURGICAL PRESS
Collegeville, Minnesota

www.litpress.org

Cover design by Monica Bokinskie. Photo courtesy of Catholic News Service/Paul Haring.

Originally published as *Homilías de Pascua* (2000–2012) © Misioneros Claretianos, 2013

Pope Francis's Easter Vigil homilies from 2014 to 2018 © Libreria Editrice Vaticana. Used with permission.

Scripture texts in this work are taken from the *New American Bible, revised edition* © 2010, 1991, 1986, 1970 Confraternity of Christian Doctrine, Washington, D.C. and are used by permission of the copyright owner. All Rights Reserved. No part of the New American Bible may be reproduced in any form without permission in writing from the copyright owner.

Excerpt from the English translation of *The Roman Missal* © 2010, International Commission on English in the Liturgy Corporation. All rights reserved.

1   2   3   4   5   6   7   8   9

Library of Congress Control Number: 2018955384

ISBN 978-0-8146-6410-0

Contents

"God Precedes Us and Loves Us First"

Homily for the Easter Vigil

METROPOLITAN CATHEDRAL, BUENOS AIRES

APRIL 22, 2000

A while ago, at the entrance to this cathedral, we proclaimed that Jesus Christ was yesterday, is today, and will always be, while we carved the numbers of this year into the paschal candle, a symbol of the risen Christ. This gesture that the church has been repeating for centuries is the bold announcement, throughout history, of what happened that Sunday morning in the cemetery in Jerusalem: the one who existed before Abraham, the one who wanted to become a companion on the journey with us, the Good Samaritan who tends to our wounds when we are beaten by life and by our fragile freedom, the one who died and was buried and sealed in his tomb—he is risen and lives forever.

This was the announcement to those women, surprised that the stone that was rolled away, from the angel sitting in the place where the dead man had been. An announcement that, from that moment, was transmitted person to person throughout the history of humanity. An announcement that boldly proclaims that, from now on, inside every death there is a seed of resurrection. The darkness we were in at the beginning of this liturgy is nothing but a symbol of sin and death. And then the light is Christ, the spark of hope that comes into our situations and our hearts, even those plunged in the greatest darkness.

The angel dispels the women's fear: "Do not be afraid" (Matt 28:5). He is talking about that instinctive fear of any hope for happiness and life, the fear that what I am seeing or what they tell me is not true, the fear of joy that is given to us is really a wasted gift. And then, after the calming reassurance not to be afraid, the sending: "Go and tell his disciples and Peter, 'He is going before you to Galilee; there you will see him, as he told you'" (Mark 16:7).

It is the Lord who always precedes us, the Lord who waits for us. The apostle John, when he wanted to explain what love is, had to resort to the experience of how it feels to be looked for, to be awaited: "In this is love: not that we have loved God, but that he loved us" first (1 John 4:10). Even if in our lives, in one way or another, we seek God, the deepest truth is that we are sought by him, we are awaited by him. Like the almond blossom mentioned by the prophets because it is the first to blossom, so it is with the Lord: he waits first, he "firsts" us in love.

For centuries our God has gone ahead of us in love. Two thousand years ago Jesus "preceded us" and awaited us in Galilee, that Galilee of the first encounter, that Galilee that each one of us has somewhere in our hearts. Our awareness of being awaited and expected quickens the pace of our walk, in order to hasten the encounter. The same God who "loved us first" is also the Good Samaritan who becomes a neighbor to us and tells us—as at the end of that parable— "Go and do likewise" (Luke 10:37). It's as simple as that: do what he did. "First" your brothers and sisters in love. Do not expect to be loved. Love first. Take the first step. Those steps that will wake us up from our drowsiness (that kept us from watching with him) or from any sophisticated quietism. A step of reconciliation, a step of love. Take the first step in your family, take the first step in this city. Become neighbor to those who live on the margins of what is necessary to survive; every day there are more. Let us imitate our God who precedes us and loves us first, by making gestures of closeness to our brothers and sisters who suffer loneliness, indigence, loss of work, exploitation, lack of shelter, disdain for being migrants, sickness, isolation in their old age. Take the first step and, by your own life, bring the announcement: he is risen. When you do you will light, in the midst of so much death, a spark of resurrection, which he wants you to bring. Then your profession of faith will be credible.

On this Easter night, I ask our Mother to help us under-stand what it means to "first" others in love. I ask her, who was awakened by hope, to help us not to be afraid to an-nounce, with our words and with our gestures of neigh-borliness toward those who are weakest, that he is alive in our midst. May she, as a good mother, lead us by the hand to the silent adoration of the God who precedes us in love. May it be so.

"Remember What He Told Us"

Homily for the Easter Vigil

METROPOLITAN CATHEDRAL, BUENOS AIRES

APRIL 15, 2001

The road traveled tonight, through centuries of promises born of the saving heart of God, culminates in a reproach and an announcement: "Why do you seek the living one among the dead? He is not here, but he has been raised" (Luke 24:5-6). It is a reproach that awakens the women from error and deception, and an announcement that redirects their lives. As the Gospel shows, it is a moment of confusion and fear for these women who, in their great love for Jesus, go out early to anoint his dead body. Confusion and fear that had already taken hold of them when "they found the stone rolled away from the tomb; but when they entered, they did not find the body of the Lord Jesus" (Luke 24:2-3).

In the midst of this confusion and fear, they receive, from angels with dazzling garments, the announcement that history has reached its fullness, that Jesus has risen. The words call them back to themselves and prompt them to look into their own hearts: "Remember what he said to you," that it was necessary for the Son of Man to be handed over and crucified, and that he would rise on the third day. "And they remembered his words" (Luke 24:6-8). The memory of Jesus' words illuminates the event, and their hearts expand—joy, admiration, a desire to run and proclaim it—and these feelings are so strong that to the disciples the women seem delirious.

Tonight we have received the announcement: Christ is risen! The Lord lives! And for us, too, the reproach is valid: "Why do you seek the living one among the dead?" There may exist, within us, a kind of impulse that leads us to close up history in sadness and failure, to shut the door of hope, to prefer to believe that the stone is rolled into place and that nobody can move it. It is true that there are existential moments in which it seems that the dawn comes only to shed light on tombs, and our lives remain imprisoned there, our search is "among the dead," among the dead things, incapable of giving life or hope. Here we are struck by that reproach: "Why do you look for the living one among the dead?" Both in our personal lives and in the society in which we live, sometimes the failures are stacked one upon the other and—sickly—we become accustomed to living among the tombs like the possessed man of the Gerasenes. Even more: we can come to believe that this is the law of life, leaving us to the fate of only thinking about what might have been but never was, and distracting us with preoccupations that help us to forget God's promise. When this happens to us, then we are sick. When this happens to our society, it becomes a sick society.

To us here today, on this Easter in Buenos Aires, the reproach is directed: "Do not look among the dead for the living one." Remember! The reproach awakens our memory, brings us the strength of the promise. We are living in a situation in which we really need our memory. Remember;

bring to our hearts the great spiritual reserve of our people, the one that was proclaimed in the moments of evangelization and that sealed in its heart in the early days the truth that Jesus is alive. Bring to mind the brotherhood that he won us with his blood, the demands of the Ten Commandments, the courage to know that sin is bad business because the devil is a bad payer, that pacts of impunity are always provisional, and that nobody laughs at God.

We are reminded to reject the solution of the high priests and elders of that time—who bribed the soldiers with "a large sum of money" (Matt 28:12) in exchange for lying and saying that the disciples had stolen the body. We are reminded that we do not walk alone in history, that we are God's family. We are asked to look around and, with the same restlessness of spirit with which the women looked for Jesus, we look for him in the face of so many of our brothers and sisters who live at the margins of indigence, of loneliness, of despair. According to how we treat them, we will be judged.

On this holy night I ask the angels to make us hear the reproaches that awaken our memory as faithful people, and to give us, in the midst of confusion and fear, the joy of hope; the hope that breaks tombs and impels the proclamation, that calls us to spend our lives generating life for others, that does not disappoint, that sometimes might make us seem delirious but that every day calls us back to ourselves as Peter returned "amazed at what had happened" (Luke 24:12). On this holy night, I ask the Virgin Mother to take us out of the quietist resignation of the cemeteries and to whisper in our ears, gently, as only mothers know how: Jesus is risen, he is alive; rouse yourself, love him, and do for your brothers and sisters what he did for you. May it be so.

"Let Us Travel the Road Together"

Homily for the Easter Vigil

METROPOLITAN CATHEDRAL, BUENOS AIRES

MARCH 20, 2002

The Gospel narrates for us the journey of these women to the tomb. They knew that Jesus was dead and walked without any doubts about this fact.

The unexpected occurs. The stone is not in front of the entrance, and the angel tells them, "Do not be afraid! . . . He has been raised." The moment becomes an event—an event that, for them, changes the meaning of life. For all of us, it changes the meaning of history. "He is going before you to Galilee; there you will see him," the angel says. They return, and on the way they encounter Jesus himself, and he gives them the same message: "Do not be afraid. Go tell my brothers to go to Galilee, and there they will see me" (Matt 28:5-10).

It seems that everything has changed direction. Instead of going to the tomb, they have to retrace their steps and return to Galilee, where they had first come to know Jesus, where they had first come to love him, where they had their first experience of awe that impelled them to exclaim, "We have

7

found the Messiah." Time had passed since those earlier moments. Time wears on things. The memory of that first encounter had been lost. As we travel through history we always run the risk of losing our memories, and he points the way: return to the memory of our first encounter; return to the memory of the first love.

The event of the resurrection of Jesus Christ invites all of us to retrace our steps—toward the first call, the first encounter, to contemplate it, now with the hope that gives the certainty of victory, the certainty of having won. Go back to that first meeting, relive it, but with the conviction that this journey was not in vain. It was a journey of the cross, but also one of victory.

And on this night I cannot stop thinking about our people today who, with sadness, are facing an immovable stone, which speaks of death, corruption, defeat. On this night we are also reminded that this is not the end of the story; that there is hope, that death, corruption, and defeat promise nothing. And tonight we are told of hope, of promise, and we are invited—to what? To retrace our steps, to reconnect with the path we have traveled as a nation.

Today each one of us is asked to look at our history, reconnect with it, in the light of the event of Jesus Christ. Today we are asked to seek forgiveness. We are asked to repair what is broken, we are asked to work in hope so that the resurrection of Christ may become a reality in each of our lives, in our entire homeland. And then to continue on our way!

And when I speak of this journey, this journey we are on, I cannot fail to mention those who have traveled farthest along this path of life: our dear elders, who are the wisdom of our people. To them I say: Do not be afraid. We know they are suffering a lot. We know that selfishness, ambition, theft, and corruption have taken away their rights and pushed them to the limit of their strength. But we also know that you can help us to retrace our steps as a nation, to harvest what you have sown. We say to you in a special way: Christ is risen. There is our hope. Take us by the hand and help us to return to the Galilee of our first love.

On this night, when a moment is transformed into an event, let us look to the strength of the resurrection of Jesus Christ, who is capable of changing things from within, capable of changing our hearts. Changing our nation. This is our hope. Let's not put it into promises that often become, in the long run, idols. How many things we have heard promised to us! How many things! Let's not be fooled. The Lord is not there in those promises.

He is risen. Retrace your steps; go to the Galilee of your first love. As a people we walk these steps, hand in hand with our elders, who are our wisdom, and there we will find that wisdom again and we will be able to be renewed as a nation. And this I ask in a special way to the one who never lost faith, she who never forgot the first love, who did not need to retrace her steps, because her path was always alive in her heart. May Mary protect us on this path to the renewal of what gives us our foundation. May it be so.

"Jesus Christ, Our Hope, Has Risen!"

Homily for the Easter Vigil

METROPOLITAN CATHEDRAL, BUENOS AIRES

APRIL 19, 2003

Mary Magdalene, Mary the mother of James, and Salome, set off at dawn on their journey. Tonight we too have traveled, following the path of the people of God along the way of election, promise, and covenant. The journey of these women is part of this long walk of centuries—and ours is, too. Because to be chosen and to be the bearers of the covenant always means to be on the move. The covenant that God makes with his people and with each one of us is precisely so that we walk toward a promise, toward an encounter. This journey is life.

In contrast, there is the stone. Immovable and sealed by the plotting of the corrupt, a solid obstacle to the encounter. These women walked, caught between the illusion and the seal. They went to the tomb to perform a work of mercy, but the reality of the stone made them doubt. They were motivated by love but paralyzed by doubt. Like them, we too feel the impulse to walk, the desire to do great works. We carry within our hearts a promise and the certainty of

10

God's faithfulness, but doubt is a stone, the bonds of corruption are chains, and often we give in to the temptation to remain paralyzed, without hope.

Paralysis sickens our soul, erases our memory, and steals our joy. It makes us forget that we have been chosen, that we are bearers of promises, that we are marked by a divine covenant. Paralysis deprives us of the surprise of the encounter, prevents us from opening ourselves to the "Good News." And today we need to hear this Good News again: "He is not here. He has been raised." We need that encounter that destroys the stones, breaks the seals, and opens a new path, that of hope.

The world needs that encounter, this world that has become like a cemetery. Our nation needs it. It needs the announcement that raises one up, the hope that motivates one to walk, the gestures of mercy, like those of the women who were going to anoint Jesus' body. We need our weakness to be anointed by hope, so that this hope will move us to proclaim the news and to anoint in solidarity the weakness of our brothers and sisters.

The worst thing that can happen to us is that we choose the stone and the corruption of the seals, that we choose the discouragement, we choose to keep quiet, forgetting that we are chosen, that we have the promise and the covenant. The worst that can happen is that our hearts are closed to the awe of the life-giving announcement that impels us to keep walking.

This is the night of the announcement. Let us shout it with all our existence: Jesus Christ, our hope, is risen! We proclaim that he is stronger than the weight of the stone and the provisional security offered by the corruption of the seals. On this night, Mary already rejoiced at the presence of her Son. To her care we entrust our desire to walk, impelled by the awe of our encounter with the risen Jesus Christ.

"I Know that My Vindicator Lives"

Homily for the Easter Vigil

METROPOLITAN CATHEDRAL, BUENOS AIRES

APRIL 10, 2004

The journey of the people of God stops tonight in front of a tomb, an empty tomb. The body of Jesus, the Son of the promise, was no longer there; only the sheets that wrapped it were visible. The pilgrimage of an entire people stops today as it once did before the rock in the desert (Exod 17:5-6) or on the shore on the night of Passover, when the Israelites, "greatly frightened . . . cried out to the LORD" (Exod 14:10) and angrily rebuked Moses, "Were there no burial places in Egypt that you brought us to die in the wilderness?" (Exod 14:11). This night is not the panic but the bewilderment (Luke 24:4) and the fear (v. 5) of these women before the incomprehensible: the Son of the promise was not there. When they return and tell everything to the apostles (v. 10), "their story seemed like nonsense and they did not believe them" (v. 11). Confusion, fear, and the appearance of delirium: these feelings are a grave, and there the centuries-long pilgrimage of an entire people stops. Confusion disorients, fear paralyzes, the appearance of delirium suggests fantasies.

The women "bowed their faces to the ground" (v. 5). Confusion and fear closes all eyes to heaven; confusion and fear without horizon, which distorts hope. They react with surprise at the reproach: "Why do you seek the living one among the dead?" (v. 5), but they are even more surprised by the prophetic word "Remember" (v. 6), and "they remembered" (v. 8). And then what was happening outside was reflected in their hearts: the breaking dawn of the day dispelled the shadows of doubt, fear, and bewilderment, and they ran and announced what they had heard: "He is not here, but he has been raised" (v. 6).

The memory resituates them in reality. They recover their memory and the awareness of being chosen people. They remember the promises, they reaffirm the covenant, and they feel newly chosen. Then that strong impetus that is of the Holy Spirit is born in the heart, to go and evangelize, to proclaim the great news. The entire history of salvation resumes. The miracle of that night in the Red Sea is repeated. "The LORD said to Moses: 'Why are you crying out to me? Tell the Israelites to set out'" (Exod 14:15). And the people continue on their way with the running of the women who had remembered the promises of the Lord.

It has happened to all of us as individuals and as a people, to find ourselves detained along the way, not knowing which way to go. In those moments it seems that the borders of life are closed, we doubt the promises, and a crass positivism presents itself as an interpretive key to the situation. Then the bewilderment and the fear overcome us; reality closes in on us, without hope, and we want to turn back and return to the same slavery that we had left. We even reproach the Lord who set us on the road to freedom: "Did we not tell you this in Egypt, when we said, 'Leave us alone that we may serve the Egyptians'? Far better for us to serve the Egyptians than to die in the wilderness" (Exod 14:12). In these situations, as on the shores of the Red Sea or in front of the tomb, the answer comes: "Do not fear!" (Exod 14:13), "Remember" (Luke 24:6).

Remember the promise but, above all, remember your own story. Remember the wonders that the Lord has done for us throughout our lives. "Be on your guard and be very careful not to forget the things your own eyes have seen, nor let them slip from your heart as long as you live" (Deut 4:9). When you are satisfied, "be careful not to forget the LORD, who brought you out of the land of Egypt, that house of slavery" (Deut 6:12). "Remember how for these forty years the LORD, your God, has directed all your journeying in the wilderness. . . . The clothing did not fall from you in tatters, nor did your feet swell" (Deut 8:2-4). "Remember the days past" (Heb 10:32). "Remember Jesus Christ, raised from the dead" (2 Tim 2:8). Thus the word of God exhorts us so that we continually re-read our history of salvation in order to be able to continue forward. The memory of the path already traveled by the grace of God is a strength and the foundation of hope to continue walking. Let us not let the memory of our salvation become atrophied by the bewilderment and fear that may come before any grave that threatens to overcome our hope. Let us always recall the word of the Lord, like the women in the sepulcher: "Remember." In moments of great darkness and paralysis, it is urgent to recover this deuteronomic dimension of existence.

On this holy night, I ask the Blessed Mother to grant us the grace to remember all the wonders that the Lord has done in our lives. May this memory shake us and impel us to continue walking in our Christian life, in the message that there is no need to look for the living one among the dead, in the message that Jesus, the Son of the promise, is the Paschal Lamb and has risen. May she tell us gently, with the certainty of one who knows that she has been led throughout her life, what she herself surely repeated that morning while waiting for her Son: "I know that my vindicator lives" (Job 19:25).

"Do Not Be Afraid!"

Homily for the Easter Vigil

METROPOLITAN CATHEDRAL, BUENOS AIRES

MARCH 26, 2005

"Behold, the veil of the sanctuary was torn in two from top to bottom. The earth quaked, rocks were split, tombs were opened. . . . The centurion and the men with him who were keeping watch over Jesus feared greatly when they saw the earthquake and all that was happening, and they said, 'Truly, this was the Son of God!'" (Matt 27:51-54). Thus with an earthquake and a spectacular commotion of earth and sky, the life of Jesus ends. He "cried out again in a loud voice, and gave up his spirit" (Matt 27:50). Then came the temporary burial because they were pressed for time, and then the silence of Saturday—that silence that penetrates body and soul, that seeps into the sorrowful wounds of the heart.

Now, "after the sabbath" (28:1), another earthquake finds Mary Magdalene and the other Mary on the way to the tomb. "And behold, there was a great earthquake; for an angel of the Lord descended from heaven, approached, rolled back the stone, and sat upon it. His appearance was like lightning and his clothing was white as snow. The guards were shaken with fear of him and became like dead men" (Matt 28:2-4).

16

Two earthquakes, two commotions of the earth, the sky, and the heart. A lot of fear and uncertainty. The first earthquake was a sort of death cry, the triumphant shout of hell in a victorious clamor of stage props. There remained the soldiers' timid confession of faith, the sorrow of those who had loved Jesus, and a warm hope . . . just embers hidden there in the depths of the soul. Embers that prompt the patience and the loving gesture of returning to the sepulcher "after the sabbath" to anoint the body of the Lord. And then, the second earthquake. Terrifying movement, but a moment of triumph. The women are frightened and the angel speaks a key word of the Gospel: "Do not be afraid. Have no fear."

"Do not be afraid," the angel had told Mary at the annunciation of the incarnation of the Word. "Do not be afraid," Jesus had repeated so many times to his disciples. It is a phrase that opens space in the soul. It is a phrase that offers security and generates hope. And immediately Jesus repeats it when he meets the women near the tomb: "Do not be afraid," it's me (Matt 28:10).

With a "have no fear," Jesus destroys the deception of the first earthquake. That first one was a cry born of the triumphalism of pride. Jesus' "do not be afraid," on the other hand, is the gentle proclamation of true triumph, the message that will be transmitted from voice to voice, from faith to faith, through the centuries. And, throughout that day, the "have no fear" will be the greeting of the risen Lord every time he meets his disciples. Thus, with that soft and powerful greeting, he returns to them the faith in the promise made. He comforts them. In Jesus' "do not be afraid," the prophecy of Isaiah is fulfilled:

> Yes, the LORD shall comfort Zion,
>   shall comfort all her ruins;

> Her wilderness he shall make like Eden,
>   her wasteland like the garden of the LORD;
> Joy and gladness shall be found in her,
>   thanksgiving and the sound of song. (51:3)

The risen Lord consoles and strengthens.

Today, on this night of true triumph, quiet and serene, the Lord again says to us, to all the faithful people: "Have no fear. I am here. I was dead and now I live." He has been repeating it for twenty centuries in each moment of triumphalist earthquake when, in his church, his passion is repeated; what is "lacking" in his suffering is "filled up" (Col 1:24). He says it in the silence of each sorrowful, anguished, disoriented heart. He says it in the confused historical circumstances when the power of the evil takes control of peoples and builds structures of sin. He says it in the arenas of all the colosseums of history. He says it in every human pain. He says it in the death of every person. "Have no fear, it's me. I am here." His definitive triumph is approaching us every time death tries to claim victory.

On this holy night, I would like all of us to be silent in our hearts and in the midst of our personal, cultural, and social earthquakes; in the midst of those earthquakes manufactured by the deception of self-sufficiency and petulance, pride and arrogance; in the midst of the earthquakes of the sin of each one of us; in the midst of all that pushes us to listen to the voice of the Lord Jesus, who was dead and is now alive, who tells us: "Do not be afraid, it's me." Accompanied by our Mother, she of tenderness and strength, let us be comforted, strengthened, and caressed by that voice of the triumphant one who repeats to us, smiling, gently, and tirelessly: "Do not be afraid, it's me."

"What Path Will My Heart Follow?"

Homily for the Easter Vigil

METROPOLITAN CATHEDRAL, BUENOS AIRES

APRIL 15, 2006

The path of these women on Sunday morning condenses the journey that the people of God made uninterruptedly from the moment Abraham began his travels "not knowing where he was to go" (Heb 11:8; cf. Gen 12:1). How many times, over the course of these centuries, the promise has been obscured by the dailiness of life, by difficulties, by wars, by exiles, deportations, and slavery! Nevertheless, the people continued to carry within themselves, often without knowing it, the seed of that promised victory. Tonight we have briefly reviewed that journey to rekindle our memory and, now with the women, we walk this stretch of loneliness and pain, of pious service to the Dead One. We already heard that they wanted to anoint the body of Jesus and that they were aware of the great difficulty that could frustrate their attempt: the stone. "It was very large," the Gospel says (Mark 16:4). And between what they intended to do and the difficulty of the stone presented, we see repeated again

Abraham's choice: they go, but without knowing where, without knowing if they can achieve their mission.

Then, the unforeseen. The worry over the stone fades upon seeing that it has been moved. The difficulty has become an entryway. Doubt looks upon a promising horizon. Surprise leads to hope. The ancient promise bursts forth in the message of the "young man": "You seek Jesus of Nazareth, the crucified. He has been raised; he is not here" (Mark 16:6). What was a wall and an obstacle becomes a new access to another certainty and another hope that puts them on the road again: "Go and tell his disciples and Peter, 'He is going before you to Galilee; there you will see him, as he told you'" (Mark 16:7).

And so a new journey begins. It is in continuity with the previous one, but it's a new one. "Go," like Abraham. And with a promise: "there you will see." We just heard that these women were far from calm: "they went out and fled from the tomb, seized with trembling and bewilderment. They . . . were afraid" (Mark 16:8). They feel the awe produced by every encounter with the Lord who, in this way, approaches them to manifest himself to them fully.

I said a moment ago that we, tonight, have recalled the great journey of our father Abraham and also the little journey of Mary Magdalene, Mary the mother of James, and Salome. And I have to ask myself: How is my journey going? Am I going in the direction of the promised encounter with the risen Jesus? Do I try to turn back out of concern for the difficulty of the stone, of the many stones of life? Or, like the pilgrims of Emmaus, do I hurry away to avoid the difficulties of a trapped heart? Or, like the other disciples, do I prefer paralysis, enclosure, defense against any news, to horizons of hope? My journey, is it a wager on hope? Do I seek the encounter? Do I know of the awe that moves one's whole being when you let yourself be moved by the Lord who passes by and opens your heart? By what path does my heart walk today?

Three journeys we saw tonight: that of the chosen people that began with our father Abraham; that of the women who, like Abraham, go in search of what they do not know; and the third: your journey and my journey. We know how the first two end: in fullness. But yours and mine, where do they go? The path? Is it quiet? Do we stop and turn back before the stone? Or do we let ourselves be touched by the news and run away from everything that is grave and death, run out trembling and shaken, because we've felt the shudder of the news and the awe of presence? I hope your heart and mine are like this. It is the best way to wish ourselves a happy Easter.

"Why Do You Look for the Living One among the Dead?"

Homily for the Easter Vigil

METROPOLITAN CATHEDRAL, BUENOS AIRES

APRIL 7, 2007

This story that we just heard was repeated every Sunday in the first Christian communities. The believers told each other the story of that Easter morning. It was a turbulent morning, with comings and goings, with uncertain emotions. A morning of jarring movements: "there was a great earthquake" (Matt 28:2), and hearts were moved with bewilderment, fear, doubt, confusion. The women who went to the tomb were afraid; the disciples were nervous. Two of them, seeking to avoid any more trouble, took off for Emmaus. Amid all of this interior and external commotion, all of the comings and goings, Jesus appears, alive, risen, and everything takes on an air of peace, joy, and happiness. The Lord "is not here, but he has been raised" (Luke 24:6), the angels had told the women . . . and finally they see him.

What was going on in the hearts of these women and of the disciples? I would like to dwell on a detail we have just heard: "But Peter got up and ran to the tomb, bent down, and saw the burial cloths alone; then he went home

amazed at what had happened" (Luke 24:12). He did not
just sit amid the questions and doubts; decisively, he ran
to see what was happening . . . and he saw for himself.
His heart knew and began to savor the awe that comes
with encountering the Lord, that combination of admiration, joy, and adoration that God gives us when he is near.
Peter gets carried away by the news and opens himself to
what he does not yet understand. There were many other
ways he could have chosen to deal with the events of that
morning, but he chooses the direct, objective path: to go
and see. He's not fooled by the confusion that arose when
the women arrived. They had proclaimed Life. And he runs
to the peripheries of death, but does not stay there, locked
in that place of tombs; having seen, he returns in awe. His
response complements the reproach that the angels spoke
to the women: "Why do you look for the living one among
the dead?" He does not allow himself to be imprisoned by
the emptiness of the grave.

"Why do you look for the living one among the dead?"
In the midst of all the circumstances and feelings of that
morning, the question marks a milestone in history. It is
directed toward the church of all times and also points to
a difference among people: there are those who choose the
grave, who insist on remaining there to search, and those
who—like Peter—open their hearts to life in the midst of
Life. How often, in our daily walk, we need to be shaken
and asked, "Why do you look for the living one among the
dead?" How often we need this question to unshackle us
from the realm of despair and death!

We need this question shouted to us every time we close
ourselves up in some form of selfishness, when we decide that
we're satisfied with the stagnant water of self-satisfaction.
We need this shouted to us when, seduced by the earthly

power that is offered to us by turning away from human and Christian values, we get drunk with the wine of the idolatry of ourselves that can only promise us a future living among the tombs. We need this shouted out to us in those moments when we put our hope in worldly vanities, in money, in fame, and we dress ourselves in the fatuous radiance of pride. We need it to be shouted to us today; our people and our culture need to hear it, so that we might open ourselves to the One who gives life, to the One who can provoke in us the hopeful awe of the encounter, the One who does not distort realities, who does not sell lies but offers only truth. How often we need the maternal tenderness of Mary to whisper to us, as if preparing the way, this victorious statement of a profound Christian strategy: "My child, do not look for the living one among the dead!"

Today, this Easter night, we need this word to be proclaimed loudly to us and for our weak and sinful hearts to be open to admiration and the awe of the encounter, so that we can hear from his lips the comforting word: "Do not be afraid. It is me."

"The Night of Encounter"

Homily for the Easter Vigil

METROPOLITAN CATHEDRAL, BUENOS AIRES

MARCH 22, 2008

In the darkness of this cathedral we have followed the steps of a long journey. God chooses a people and puts them on the road. It begins with Abraham: "Go forth from your land, your relatives, and from your father's house to a land I will show you. I will make of you a great nation" (Gen 12:1-2). Abraham left and became the father of a people who made history on the road, a people walking toward the promise. We have also just traveled along as we listened to this story of a journey through lands and through centuries, with our eyes fixed on the paschal candle, the definitive Promise made real, the living Christ, conqueror of death, risen. Life in God is not quiet; it is a life in movement. And even God himself set out, in search of humanity . . . and so became human. On this night we have traveled the two paths: that of the people, of humanity to God, and that of God to humanity, both paths making possible an encounter. The longing for God sown in our human heart, that yearning for God given as a promise to Abraham and, on the other hand, the longing of God's own heart, his boundless love for us, encounter each other here tonight, before this paschal candle, symbol of the risen Christ. Here the searches and the longings, the desires and the loves, are resolved; we encounter the risen Christ, the goal and the triumph of both journeys. This is the night of the encounter . . . of the "Encounter," with a capital E.

It is striking how the Gospel that we have just heard describes the encounter of the victorious Jesus Christ with the women. Nothing is quiet, and everyone is on the move: the women are walking, the earth trembles powerfully, the angel comes down from heaven and rolls the stone away, the guards tremble in fear. Then the invitation: he will be in Galilee; everyone go to Galilee. The women, with that mixture of fear and joy—that is to say, with their hearts on the move—go off quickly and run to break the news. They meet Jesus and they approach him and they embrace his feet. The movement of the women toward Christ, the movement of Christ toward them. From this movement comes an encounter.

The Gospel message is not relegated to a distant history that happened two thousand years ago. It is a reality that continues to play out every time we set out on God's path and let ourselves be found by him. The Gospel captures a moment of encounter, of victorious encounter between the faithful God, passionate for his people, and us, sinners, but thirsting for love and searching, having agreed to set out on the road . . . to set out on the road to find him . . . to let ourselves be found by him. In this moment, existential and temporal, we experience what the women did: fear and joy at the same time, that awe of encountering Jesus Christ, who fulfills our desires, but who never says "stay," but always "go." The encounter prepares us. It strengthens our identity and sends us on. It puts us on the road so that, from encounter to encounter, we will reach the definitive encounter.

I pointed out that, in the midst of the darkness, our eyes have been focused on the paschal candle, Christ, reality and hope at the same time; reality of an encounter today and hope of the great final encounter. This is good for us because we live in the midst of failed encounters (*desencuentros*) daily. We have become accustomed to living in a culture of failed encounters, in which our passions, disorientations, enmities, and conflicts confront us, separate us, isolate us, and harden us into that sterile individualism that is proposed to us as a way of life every day. The women, that morning, were victims of a painful failed encounter: their Lord had been taken away. They were alone before a tomb. This is where the cultural proposal of today's paganism leaves us in the world and in our city: alone, still, at the end of a journey of illusion that becomes a tomb, dead in our sterile frustration and selfishness. Today we need the power of God to move us. We need a great earthquake, an angel to roll away the stone in our hearts that blocks our journey, with lightning and a lot of light. Today we need our souls to be shaken, to be told that the idolatry of "cultured" and possessive quietism does not give life. Today, having been shaken by many frustrations, we need to encounter him again and hear him say to us: Do not be afraid. Get back on the path. Return to the Galilee of your first love.

We need to resume the journey that our father Abraham began and that this paschal candle points us to. Today we need to encounter Christ—for us to encounter him and for him to encounter us. Brothers and sisters, the "happy Easter" that I wish for you is that today an angel will roll the stone away and let us encounter him. May it be so.

"The Stone Has Been Moved"

Homily for the Easter Vigil

METROPOLITAN CATHEDRAL, BUENOS AIRES

APRIL 11, 2009

These good women got up early to go anoint Jesus' dead body. They loved him very much. They were convinced: he's dead. It's over. The story is over. A lovely fantasy is over. We have to face life and continue as we can. But love led them to that. And they were there worried about who was going to open the tomb, who would move the round stone that had been pushed into place to cover the door of the tomb. They were worried about that. They were chatting: "Who will roll back the stone for us?" (Mark 16:3). The Gospel tells us, "It was very large" (v. 4). The rest we know: they found the stone removed, the angel announced that Jesus was alive, and then they ran away trembling, without saying anything to anyone, because they were scared to death.

I thought, when I heard the Gospel, about all the centuries of history that we have relived here today with the readings from the history of salvation, of the Jewish people, of the people of God . . . all those centuries of history crash into a stone that seems immovable by anyone. All the promises of the prophets, the dreams, the hopes—they end there, smashed on a stone. And I thought we could move from thinking of the centuries of history to consider our own lives. We each have our own history. Not centuries. But years and years of stories, with their pros and their cons, their goods and their bads, we each have our own. And we each have our faith in Jesus.

But I wonder: How often is our Christian life, our life of following Jesus, nothing more than worrying about who is going to move a stone? And that's how we spend our lives! Whether this can be done or that can't be done, how can I be more good, how can I be better, or how can I fix this or that other thing . . . always in front of a stone! That I know I can't move! And that binds us, it takes away our freedom. It keeps us from flying! It keeps us from being us! And I would even say it blurs our name. How many hours, days, weeks, months, and years thinking about who is going to move the stone. That is a shame.

When they tell us, "See, the stone is removed, the one you are looking for is alive right there next to you," at that point we are seized by fear and we run off! We prefer the security of just having to think about who is going to move the stone. We prefer that to the insecurity of his being alive and with us, inspiring us in new, bold, and creative ways with every new moment, the insecurity of being inspired by the life of the risen One.

Today, as we consider the thoughts of these women, let's also ask ourselves about the thoughts of our own lives. Let's ask ourselves if we are convinced that the stone has already been rolled away and that there is no one inside. "Yes Father, we are all convinced." Okay then, if you are convinced, tell me, why waste time worrying about who is going to take away the difficulty? You have him alive with you! He is risen! He is alive! He is with us! Instead of feeling sadness at the thought of who is going to move the stone of the difficulty, feel the awe of the encounter with him, that awe that transforms you, that awe that changes your life!

And tonight we ask Jesus, each one of us asks for ourselves and for all of us here: "Lord, let us feel the awe of encountering you. Keep our lives from remaining entangled in secondary matters, concerned about this thing or that thing, whether I can or can't. Help me to feel the joy, the admiration, the happiness, the awe of knowing you are risen, alive, at my side, and that this is not a fiction.

We have two paths to choose from: either we believe in the stone that is covering the tomb and we worry about who is going to move it, or we believe that he has already left the tomb and is accompanying us. What we celebrate today is the second way: he is alive. May we encounter him. May we allow ourselves to encounter him in a way that changes our lives. May it be so.

"Holding on to the Rope of Hope"

Homily for the Easter Vigil

METROPOLITAN CATHEDRAL, BUENOS AIRES

APRIL 3, 2010

We hear this passage from the Gospel of Luke and find a mixture of feelings on that Sunday morning: the women were troubled because they saw the tomb open, they were full of fear, they didn't dare to look up from the ground. When they returned from the tomb, they told this to the eleven, who thought the women were delirious. They didn't believe them. Peter goes to see and returns in amazement. Anxiety, fear, delirium . . . all these feelings are mixed up in the Gospel story that we have just heard. They were caught up in a situation they didn't understand! That they could not interpret! A situation whose meaning they could not grasp. And added to that, there's an angel who says to them, "Why do you seek the living one among the dead?" And the angel has to explain to them, "Remember what he said to you while he was still in Galilee, that the Son of Man must be handed over to sinners and be crucified, and rise on the third day" (Luke 24:6-7). Then the women remembered his words.

These women and the disciples were imprisoned because they had *forgotten*. They had *forgotten* the word of the Lord, and they needed an angel to shake them and tell them: Remember the promise and take hope! The women and these disciples are the first Christians without hope that appear in history. They had lost hope in their Lord because they had forgotten his prophecy, they had forgotten his promise. Then they became entangled in the dynamics of the situation. It is so easy to fall into this trap, so easy to become a Christian without hope: I am a Christian, I go to Mass on Sundays but . . . Do you think Jesus is alive in your midst? In the midst of your family? In your life? Do you walk with the living Lord? Ah . . . good . . . yes, of course . . . we buried everything and we continued walking as if the Lord were buried and the stone still firmly fixed in front of the tomb. And the voice of the angel, who shakes us back to our senses: "Why do you seek the living one among the dead?" You will not get anywhere going along this path! If you do not remember the prophecy, if you forget what Jesus himself told you, you will not have hope and you will be a prisoner of the situation, of the terror of the moment, of the convenience of the moment, of fear, of the disbelief of the moment.

Saint Peter told the first Christians that they ought to be ready to give a reason for their hope, that they ought to have the courage to say: "I take this path because I hope! I hope that this Lord who is alive walking with me will bring the fullness of my life and of the whole world when he comes a second time. I take this path, I behave like this because I know the Lord will come! And I want him to find me watching, waiting in hope." This hope is based on the memory of Jesus' promise: "I am going to be resurrected and I will be with you every day until the end of the world." Do I really believe this is so?

I wish you this Easter a renewal of your memory, a renewal of the memory of each of us. The memory of what Jesus proclaimed about himself, and that in that memory we may find hope and walk in hope, which is not the same as walking in optimism. Optimism is a psychological attitude; hope is a gift from God, the virtue that God puts in your heart and that keeps you rooted in the promise of God, keeps you from losing your way. Hope is that anchor that is thrown to the edges of the fullness of time and we grab the rope of that anchor so as not to become disoriented amid the various hopeless, pessimistic, or simply neutral ideas that life puts in our hearts, that do not satisfy us to our depths and that leave us sad like someone stumbling around lost.

Holding on to this rope of hope, with the memory of what Jesus promised us, let us move forward and remember what the angel tells us: "Do not look for the living one among the dead." May it be so.

"Today I Put Before You Life"

Homily for the Easter Vigil

METROPOLITAN CATHEDRAL, BUENOS AIRES

APRIL 23, 2011

Sunday was dawning as these women who loved Jesus so much went to visit the tomb—that tomb they had been sitting in front of (cf. Matt 27:61) the previous Friday, contemplating the burial of the Lord; that tomb they'd had to leave because the Sabbath rest prescribed by the Law had begun (cf. John 19:42); that tomb, closed up with that stone that Joseph of Arimathea had rolled in front of it and which those who wrestled with a bad conscience had ordered secured and sealed (cf. Matt 27:66); that stone that had definitively killed the expectations of salvation that had been created with the life and preaching of Jesus; that stone—secured, sealed, and watched by the guards—that made so many promises seem like lies. The stone announced a blunt failure, and those dispirited women walked sadly toward that monument to failure.

And then God says, "Enough!" The earthquakes, and the angel of the Lord with the shining force of a new truth rolls the stone away. That empty tomb lies open. And the angel says to the women, "He is not here, for he has been raised just as he said" (Matt 28:6). Then they remembered.

34

They remembered that little spark of hope whose place in their hearts they had given up. From here on, we who are followers of Jesus know that beyond a grave there is always hope, that the stone of our self-sufficiency cannot match the power of God in the tortured and restored flesh of his Son Jesus. They had wanted to "assure" death, and—without knowing it or believing it—they assured life to all humanity.

Before this stone that has been moved away, different feelings arise. The guards tremble in terror and become "like dead men" (Matt 28:4). The women are terrified but the message of the angel fills them with joy and "they went away quickly from the tomb" (Matt 28:8). The guards are paralyzed by their loyalty to death, but the message of life fills the women with hope and gives them joy, a joy that impels them to hurry to break the news. Death paralyzes; life provides the impulse to communicate it.

The women are bearers of news: Jesus hadn't lied, he was alive and they had seen him. The guards, petrified in their existential narrowness, only manage to concentrate on the quick and temporary protection of the bribe. Thus the biblical text continues: "While they were going, some of the guard went into the city and told the chief priests all that had happened. They assembled with the elders and took counsel; then they gave a large sum of money to the soldiers, telling them, 'You are to say, "His disciples came by night and stole him while we were asleep." And if this gets to the ears of the governor, we will satisfy him and keep you out of trouble.' The soldiers took the money and did as they were instructed" (Matt 28:11-15).

Contemplating the difference in the feelings of the women and the guards, we who are here today, celebrating the new Life that the risen Jesus offers and gives us, have to ask ourselves: What attracts us more—the safety of the sealed tomb, or the joyful insecurity of the message? Where is our heart—in the certainty offered to us by dead things, without a future, or in that joy in hope of those who bear news of life? Do we run after Life with the promise of finding it in that Galilee of the encounter, or do we prefer the existential bribe that protects any stone that closes and annuls our heart? Do I prefer sadness or a simple paralyzing contentment, or do I push myself toward joy, that path of joy that springs from the conviction that my Redeemer lives?

Moses, before he died, gathered the people and said: "I have today set before you life and good [or] death and evil" (Deut 30:15). Today, too, in this liturgical celebration with the risen Jesus really present at the altar, the church proposes something similar to us: either we believe in the power of the tomb closed by the stone, adopting it as a way of life and feeding our heart with sadness, or we open ourselves to receive the announcement of the angel—"He is not here, for he has been raised"—and we accept joy, that "sweet and comforting joy of evangelizing" that impels us to proclaim that he is alive and awaits each one of us, at every moment, in the Galilee of the encounter.

May the Holy Spirit teach us and help us to choose well.

"The Night Will Shine
Like the Day"

Homily for the Easter Vigil

METROPOLITAN CATHEDRAL, BUENOS AIRES

APRIL 7, 2012

At dawn they left their house to go to the tomb. They had already bought the perfumes to anoint the body of Jesus. Preparing everything, they had practically stayed up all night, until there was enough light to go as soon as the sun came up. We too are awake tonight, not preparing to anoint the Lord's body, but remembering the wonders of God in the history of humanity. Mainly we remember that the Lord also spent the night of the great wonders awake: "This was a night of vigil for the LORD, when he brought them out of the land of Egypt" (Exod 12:42). This vigil of ours responds to a command of gratitude: "so on this night all Israelites must keep a vigil for the LORD throughout their generations" (ibid).

Just as happens during the Israelites' annual remembrance, it is possible that our children, our acquaintances, will ask us the reason for doing it. The answer must come from the depths of our memory as the chosen people of the Lord: "With a strong hand the LORD brought us out of Egypt, out of a house of slavery" (Exod 13:14). So it does:

This is the night,
when once you led our forebears, Israel's children,
from slavery in Egypt
and made them pass dry-shod through the Red Sea.

This is the night
that with a pillar of fire
banished the darkness of sin. . . .

This is the night,
when Christ broke the prison-bars of death
and rose victorious from the underworld. . . .

This is the night
of which it is written:
The night shall be as bright as day . . . (*The Exsultet*)

In the light of what we celebrate in this vigil, our life will continue, and what happened to our forebears in the desert will happen to us, too. Many times the difficulties, the distractions of the journey, and the pains and sorrows of life obscure the joy and even the certainty of the freedom we have been given, and we can begin to long for the "nice things" that we had in slavery, the garlic and onions back in Egypt (see Num 11:4-6). We too can be overcome by impatience and wish to opt for the short-term immediacy of idols (see Exod 32:1-6). In those moments, it seems, the sun hides, the night returns, and the freedom we were given is eclipsed.

To Mary Magdalene, Mary the mother of James, and Salome, just as the day dawned, another night came upon them, a night of fear, and they "fled from the tomb" (Mark 16:8). They ran away without saying anything to anyone. Fear made them forget what they had just heard: "You seek Jesus of Nazareth, the crucified. He has been raised; he is not here" (Mark 16:6). Fear silenced them, so they could not proclaim the news. Fear paralyzed their hearts and they got stuck in the safety of a secure failure instead of opening themselves to hope, the hope that told them, "He is going before you to Galilee; there you will see him" (Mark 16:7).

The same also happens to us; we are afraid of hope and prefer to bask in our limitations, in our pettiness and sins, in the doubts and denials that, good or bad, we at least know we're able to handle. They came in mourning, they came to anoint a corpse . . . and they hold on to that; just as the disciples of Emmaus are locked in disappointment (see Luke 24:13-24). Deep down, they were afraid of joy (cf. Luke 24:41).

And history repeats itself. On those nights of ours, nights of fear, nights of temptation and trial, nights when we want to return to the slavery we left behind, the Lord keeps watch with us as he did that night in Egypt. And with sweet and fatherly words he tells us, "Why are you troubled? And why do questions arise in your hearts? Look at my hands and my feet, that it is I myself. Touch me and see" (Luke 24:38-39). Or sometimes, with a little more energy, "Oh, how foolish you are! How slow of heart to believe all that the prophets spoke! Was it not necessary that the Messiah should suffer these things and enter into his glory?" (Luke 24:25-26). The risen Lord is always alive by our side.

Every time God manifested himself to an Israelite, he tried to dispel that person's fear: "Do not be afraid," he would say. Jesus does the same: "Do not be afraid." It is what the angel tells these three women who were compelled by fear to opt for the wake. Let's say to each other on this night of vigil: Do not be afraid, do not fear. We must turn down the offer of certainty; we must not turn away from hope. Let us not opt for the security of the grave, in this case not empty but full of the rebellious filth of our sins and selfishness. Let us open ourselves to the gift of hope. Do not fear the joy of the resurrection of Christ.

On that night, she too, the Mother, was awake. She could sense in her heart the nearness of that life she had conceived in Nazareth, and her faith confirmed the intuition. We ask her, as the first disciple, to teach us to persevere in the vigil, to accompany us in patience, to strengthen us in hope. We ask her to lead us to encounter her risen Son. We ask her to free us from fear, so that we can hear the announcement of the angel and also run—not to run away in fright, but to run to announce the Good News to others in this city of Buenos Aires that needs it so much.

"Let Us Be Open
to the Newness of God"

Homily for the Easter Vigil

ST. PETER'S BASILICA, THE VATICAN

MARCH 30, 2013

In the Gospel of this radiant night of the Easter Vigil, we first meet the women who go to the tomb of Jesus with spices to anoint his body (cf. Luke 24:1-3). They go to perform an act of compassion, a traditional act of affection and love for a dear, departed person, just as we would. They had followed Jesus, they had listened to his words, they had felt understood by him in their dignity, and they had accompanied him to the very end, to Calvary and to the moment when he was taken down from the cross. We can imagine their feelings as they make their way to the tomb: a certain sadness, sorrow that Jesus had left them, he had died, his life had come to an end. Life would now go on as before. Yet the women continued to feel love, the love for Jesus that now led them to his tomb. But at this point, something completely new and unexpected happens, something that upsets their hearts and their plans, something that will upset their whole life: they see the stone removed from before the tomb, they draw near, and they do not find the Lord's body.

41

It is an event that leaves them perplexed, hesitant, full of questions: "What happened?" "What is the meaning of all this?" (cf. Luke 24:4). Doesn't the same thing also happen to us when something completely new occurs in our everyday life? We stop short, we don't understand, we don't know what to do. Newness often makes us fearful, including the newness that God brings us, the newness that God asks of us. We are like the apostles in the Gospel: often we would prefer to hold on to our own security, to stand in front of a tomb, to think about someone who has died, someone who ultimately lives on only as a memory, like the great historical figures from the past. We are afraid of God's surprises. Dear brothers and sisters, we are afraid of God's surprises! He always surprises us! The Lord is like that.

Dear brothers and sisters, let us not be closed to the newness that God wants to bring into our lives! Are we often weary, disheartened, and sad? Do we feel weighed down by our sins? Do we think that we won't be able to cope? Let us not close our hearts, let us not lose confidence, let us never give up: there are no situations that God cannot change; there is no sin that he cannot forgive if only we open ourselves to him.

But let us return to the Gospel, to the women, and take one step further. They find the tomb empty, the body of Jesus is not there, something new has happened, but all this still doesn't tell them anything certain: it raises questions; it leaves them confused, without offering an answer. And suddenly there are two men in dazzling clothes who say: "Why do you look for the living among the dead? He is not here; but has risen" (Luke 24:5-6). What was a simple act, done surely out of love—going to the tomb—has now turned into an event, a truly life-changing event. Nothing remains as it was before, not only in the lives of those women, but also in our own lives and in the history of mankind. Jesus is not dead, he has risen, he is alive! He does not simply return to life; rather, he is life itself, because he is the Son of God, the living God (cf. Num 14:21-28; Deut 5:26; Josh 3:10). Jesus no longer belongs to the past, but lives in the present and is projected toward the future; Jesus is the everlasting "today" of God. This is how the newness of God appears to the women, the disciples, and all of us: as victory over sin, evil, and death, over everything that crushes life and makes it seem less human. And this is a message meant for me and for you dear sister, for you dear brother. How often does Love have to tell us: Why do you look for the living among the dead? Our daily problems and worries can wrap us up in ourselves, in sadness and bitterness . . . and that is where death is. That is not the place to look for the One who is alive! Let the risen Jesus enter your life, welcome him as a friend, with trust: he is life! If up till now you have kept him at a distance, step forward. He will receive you with open arms. If you have been indifferent, take a risk: you won't be disappointed. If following him seems difficult, don't be afraid, trust him, be confident that he is close to you—he is with you and he will give you the peace you are looking for and the strength to live as he would have you do.

There is one last little element that I would like to emphasize in the Gospel for this Easter Vigil. The women encounter the newness of God. Jesus has risen, he is alive! But faced with empty tomb and the two men in brilliant clothes, their first reaction is one of fear: "they were terrified and bowed their faces to the ground," Saint Luke tells us—they didn't even have courage to look. But when they hear the message of the resurrection, they accept it in faith. And the two men in dazzling clothes tell them something of crucial importance: remember. "Remember what he told you when he was still in Galilee . . . And they remembered his words" (Luke 24:6, 8). This is the invitation to remember their encounter with Jesus, to remember his words, his actions, his life; and it is precisely this loving remembrance of their experience with the Master that enables the women to master their fear and to bring the message of the resurrection to the apostles and all the others (cf. Luke 24:9). To remember what God has done and continues to do for me, for us, to remember the road we have travelled; this is what opens our hearts to hope for the future. May we learn to remember everything that God has done in our lives.

On this radiant night, let us invoke the intercession of the Virgin Mary, who treasured all these events in her heart (cf. Luke 2:19, 51) and ask the Lord to give us a share in his resurrection. May he open us to the newness that transforms, to the beautiful surprises of God. May he make us men and women capable of remembering all that he has done in our own lives and in the history of our world. May he help us to feel his presence as the one who is alive and at work in our midst. And may he teach us each day, dear brothers and sisters, not to look among the dead for the living One. Amen.

"Return to Galilee!"

Homily for the Easter Vigil

ST. PETER'S BASILICA, THE VATICAN

APRIL 19, 2014

The Gospel of the resurrection of Jesus Christ begins with the journey of the women to the tomb at dawn on the day after the Sabbath. They go to the tomb to honor the body of the Lord, but they find it open and empty. A mighty angel says to them: "Do not be afraid!" (Matt 28:5) and orders them to go and tell the disciples: "He has been raised from the dead, and indeed he is going ahead of you to Galilee" (v. 7). The women quickly depart and on the way Jesus himself meets them and says: "Do not fear; go and tell my brothers to go to Galilee; there they will see me" (v. 10). "Do not be afraid," "do not fear": these are words that encourage us to open our hearts to receive the message.

After the death of the Master, the disciples had scattered; their faith had been utterly shaken, everything seemed over, all their certainties had crumbled and their hopes had died. But now that message of the women, incredible as it was, came to them like a ray of light in the darkness. The news spread: Jesus is risen as he said. And then there was his command to go to *Galilee*; the women had heard it twice, first from the angel and then from Jesus himself: "Let them

go to Galilee; there they will see me." "Do not fear" and
"go to Galilee."

Galilee is *the place where they were first called, where
everything began!* To return there, to return to the place
where they were originally called. Jesus had walked along
the shores of the lake as the fishermen were casting their
nets. He had called them, and they left everything and
followed him (cf. Matt 4:18-22).

To return to Galilee means *to re-read* everything on
the basis of the cross and its victory, fearlessly: "do not be
afraid." To re-read everything—Jesus' preaching, his mira-
cles, the new community, the excitement and the defections,
even the betrayal—to re-read everything starting from the
end, which is a new beginning, *from this supreme act of love.*

For each of us, too, there is a "Galilee" at the origin of
our journey with Jesus. "To go to Galilee" means something
beautiful; it means rediscovering our baptism as a living
fountainhead, drawing new energy from the sources of our
faith and our Christian experience. To return to Galilee
means above all to return to that blazing light with which
God's grace touched me at the start of the journey. From
that flame I can light a fire for today and every day, and
bring heat and light to my brothers and sisters. That flame
ignites a humble joy, a joy that sorrow and distress cannot
dismay, a good, gentle joy.

In the life of every Christian, after baptism there is also
another "Galilee," *a more existential "Galilee"*: the experience of a *personal encounter with Jesus Christ* who called
me to follow him and to share in his mission. In this sense,
returning to Galilee means treasuring in my heart the living
memory of that call, when Jesus passed my way, gazed at
me with mercy and asked me to follow him. To return there
means reviving the memory of that moment when his eyes

met mine, the moment when he made me realize that he loved me.

Today, tonight, each of us can ask: *What is my Galilee?* I need to remind myself to go back and remember. *Where is my Galilee?* Do I remember it? Have I forgotten it? Seek and you will find it! There the Lord is waiting for you. Have I gone off on roads and paths that made me forget it? Lord, help me: tell me what my Galilee is; for you know that I want to return there to encounter you and to let myself be embraced by your mercy. Do not be afraid, do not fear, return to Galilee!

The Gospel is very clear: we need to go back there, to see Jesus risen, and to become witnesses of his resurrection. This is not to go back in time; it is not a kind of nostalgia. It is returning to our first love, in order to *receive the fire* Jesus has kindled in the world and to bring that fire to all people, to the very ends of the earth. Go back to Galilee, without fear! "Galilee of the Gentiles" (Matt 4:15; Isa 8:23)! Horizon of the risen Lord, horizon of the church; intense desire of encounter . . . Let us be on our way!

"To Enter into the Mystery"

Homily for the Easter Vigil

ST. PETER'S BASILICA, THE VATICAN

APRIL 4, 2015

Tonight is a night of vigil. The Lord is not sleeping; the Watchman is watching over his people (cf. Ps 121:4), to bring them out of slavery and to open before them the way to freedom.

The Lord is keeping watch and, by the power of his love, he is bringing his people through the Red Sea. He is also bringing Jesus through the abyss of death and the netherworld.

This was a night of vigil for the disciples of Jesus, a night of sadness and fear. The men remained locked in the Upper Room. Yet the women went to the tomb at dawn on Sunday to anoint Jesus' body. Their hearts were overwhelmed and they were asking themselves: "How will we enter? Who will roll back the stone of the tomb? . . ." But here was the first sign of the great event: the large stone was already rolled back and the tomb was open!

"Entering the tomb, they saw a young man sitting on the right side, dressed in a white robe . . ." (Mark 16:5). The women were the first to see this great sign, the empty tomb; and they were the first to enter. . . .

"Entering the tomb." It is good for us, on this Vigil night, to reflect on the experience of the women, which also speaks to us. For that is why we are here: to enter, to enter into the mystery God has accomplished with his vigil of love.

We cannot live Easter without entering into the mystery. It is not something intellectual, something we only know or read about . . . It is more, much more!

"To enter into the mystery" means the ability to wonder, to contemplate; the ability to listen to the silence and to hear the tiny whisper amid great silence by which God speaks to us (cf. 1 Kgs 19:12).

To enter into the mystery demands that we not be afraid of reality: that we not be locked into ourselves, that we not flee from what we fail to understand, that we not close our eyes to problems or deny them, that we not dismiss our questions. . . .

To enter into the mystery means going beyond our own comfort zone, beyond the laziness and indifference that hold us back, and going out in search of truth, beauty, and love. It is seeking a deeper meaning, an answer, and not an easy one, to the questions that challenge our faith, our fidelity, and our very existence.

To enter into the mystery, we need humility, the lowliness to abase ourselves, to come down from the pedestal of our "I," which is so proud, of our presumption; the humility not to take ourselves so seriously, recognizing who we really are: creatures with strengths and weaknesses, sinners in need of forgiveness. To enter into the mystery we need the lowliness that is powerlessness, the renunciation of our idols . . . in a word, we need to adore. Without adoration, we cannot enter into the mystery.

The women who were Jesus' disciples teach us all of this. They kept watch that night, together with Mary. And she,

the Virgin Mother, helped them not to lose faith and hope.
As a result, they did not remain prisoners of fear and sadness, but at the first light of dawn they went out carrying their ointments, their hearts anointed with love. They went forth and found the tomb open. And they went in. They had kept watch, they went forth, and they entered into the mystery. May we learn from them to keep watch with God and with Mary our Mother, so that we too may enter into the mystery, which leads from death to life.

"Receiving the Gift of Hope"

Homily for the Easter Vigil

ST. PETER'S BASILICA, THE VATICAN

MARCH 26, 2016

"Peter . . . ran to the tomb" (Luke 24:12). What thoughts crossed Peter's mind and stirred his heart as he ran to the tomb? The Gospel tells us that the eleven, including Peter, had not believed the testimony of the women, their Easter proclamation. Quite the contrary, "these words seemed to them an idle tale" (v. 11). Thus there was doubt in Peter's heart, together with many other worries: sadness at the death of the beloved Master and disillusionment for having denied him three times during his passion.

There is, however, something that signals a change in him: after listening to the women and refusing to believe them, "Peter rose" (v. 12). He did not remain sedentary, in thought; he did not stay at home as the others did. He did not succumb to the somber atmosphere of those days, nor was he overwhelmed by his doubts. He was not consumed by remorse, fear, or the continuous gossip that leads nowhere. He was looking for Jesus, not himself. He preferred the path of encounter and trust. And so, he got up, just as he was, and ran toward the tomb from where he would return "amazed" (v. 12). This marked the beginning of Peter's resurrection, the resurrection of his heart. Without giving in to sadness or darkness, he made room for hope: he allowed the light of God to enter into his heart, without smothering it.

The women too, who had gone out early in the morning to perform a work of mercy, taking the perfumed ointments to the tomb, had the same experience. They were "frightened and bowed their faces," and yet they were deeply affected by the words of the angel: "Why do you seek the living one among the dead?" (v. 5).

We, like Peter and the women, cannot discover life by being sad, bereft of hope. Let us not stay imprisoned within ourselves, but let us break open our sealed tombs to the Lord—each of us knows what they are—so that he may enter and grant us life. Let us give him the stones of our rancor and the boulders of our past, those heavy burdens of our weaknesses and falls. Christ wants to come and take us by the hand to bring us out of our anguish. This is the first stone to be moved aside this night: the lack of hope that imprisons us within ourselves. May the Lord free us from this trap, from being Christians without hope, who live as if the Lord were not risen, as if our problems were the center of our lives.

We see and will continue to see problems both within and without. They will always be there. But tonight it is important to shed the light of the risen Lord upon our problems, and in a certain sense, to "evangelize" them. To evangelize our problems. Let us not allow darkness and fear to distract us and control us; we must cry out to them: the Lord "is not here, but has risen!" (v. 6). He is our greatest joy; he is always at our side and will never let us down.

This is the foundation of our hope, which is not mere optimism, nor a psychological attitude or desire to be courageous. Christian hope is a gift that God gives us if we come out of ourselves and open our hearts to him. This hope does not disappoint us because the Holy Spirit has been poured into our hearts (cf. Rom 5:5). The Paraclete does not make everything look appealing. He does not remove evil with a magic wand. But he pours into us the vitality of life, which is not the absence of problems, but the certainty of being loved and always forgiven by Christ, who for us has conquered sin, conquered death, and conquered fear. Today is the celebration of our hope, the celebration of this truth: nothing and no one will ever be able to separate us from his love (cf. Rom 8:39).

The Lord is alive and wants to be sought among the living. After having found him, each person is sent out by him to announce the Easter message, to awaken and resurrect hope in hearts burdened by sadness, in those who struggle to find meaning in life. This is so necessary today. However, we must not proclaim ourselves. Rather, as joyful servants of hope, we must announce the risen One by our lives and by our love; otherwise we will be only an international organization full of followers and good rules, yet incapable of offering the hope for which the world longs.

How can we strengthen our hope? The liturgy of this night offers some guidance. It teaches us to remember the works of God. The readings describe God's faithfulness, the history of his love toward us. The living word of God is able to involve us in this history of love, nourishing our hope and renewing our joy. The Gospel also reminds us of this: in order to kindle hope in the hearts of the women, the angel tells them: "Remember what [Jesus] told you" (v. 6). Remember the words of Jesus, remember all that he has done in our lives. Let us not forget his words and his works; otherwise we will lose hope and become "hopeless" Christians. Let us instead remember the Lord, his goodness and his life-giving words, which have touched us. Let us remember them and make them ours, to be sentinels of the morning who know how to help others see the signs of the risen Lord.

Dear brothers and sisters, Christ is risen! And we have the possibility of opening our hearts and receiving his gift of hope. Let us open our hearts to hope and go forth. May the memory of his works and his words be the bright star directing our steps in the ways of faith toward that Easter that will have no end.

"The Heartbeat
of the Risen Lord"

Homily for the Easter Vigil

ST. PETER'S BASILICA, THE VATICAN

APRIL 15, 2017

"After the sabbath, as the first day of the week was dawning, Mary Magdalene and the other Mary went to see the tomb" (Matt 28:1). We can picture them as they went on their way . . . They walked like people going to a cemetery, with uncertain and weary steps, like those who find it hard to believe that this is how it all ended. We can picture their faces, pale and tearful. And their question: can Love have truly died?

Unlike the disciples, the women are present—just as they had been present as the Master breathed his last on the cross, and then, with Joseph of Arimathea, as he was laid in the tomb. Two women who did not run away, who remained steadfast, who faced life as it is, and who knew the bitter taste of injustice. We see them there, before the tomb, filled with grief but equally incapable of accepting that things must always end this way.

If we try to imagine this scene, we can see in the faces of those women any number of other faces: the faces of

55

mothers and grandmothers, of children and young people who bear the grievous burden of injustice and brutality. In their faces we can see reflected all those who, walking the streets of our cities, feel the pain of dire poverty, the sorrow born of exploitation and human trafficking. We can also see the faces of those who are greeted with contempt because they are immigrants, deprived of country, house, and family. We see faces whose eyes bespeak loneliness and abandonment, because their hands are creased with wrinkles. Their faces mirror the faces of women, mothers, who weep as they see the lives of their children crushed by massive corruption that strips them of their rights and shatters their dreams. By daily acts of selfishness that crucify and then bury people's hopes. By paralyzing and barren bureaucracies that stand in the way of change. In their grief, those two women reflect the faces of all those who, walking the streets of our cities, behold human dignity crucified.

The faces of those women mirror many other faces too, including perhaps yours and mine. Like them, we can feel driven to keep walking and not resign ourselves to the fact that things have to end this way. True, we carry within us a promise and the certainty of God's faithfulness. But our faces also bear the mark of wounds, of so many acts of infidelity, our own and those of others, of efforts made and battles lost. In our hearts, we know that things can be different but, almost without noticing it, we can grow accustomed to living with the tomb, living with frustration. Worse, we can even convince ourselves that this is the law of life, and blunt our consciences with forms of escape that only serve to dampen the hope that God has entrusted to us. So often we walk as those women did, poised between the desire of God and bleak resignation. Not only does the Master die, but our hope dies with him.

"And suddenly there was a great earthquake" (Matt 28:2). Unexpectedly, those women felt a powerful tremor, as something or someone made the earth shake beneath their feet. Once again, someone came to tell them: "Do not be afraid," but now adding: "He has been raised as he said!" This is the message that, generation after generation, this holy night passes on to us: "Do not be afraid, brothers and sisters; he is risen as he said!" Life, which death destroyed on the cross, now reawakens and pulsates anew (cf. Romano Guardini, *The Lord*, Chicago, 1954, p. 473). The heartbeat of the risen Lord is granted us as a gift, a present, a new horizon. The beating heart of the risen Lord is given to us, and we are asked to give it in turn as a transforming force, as the leaven of a new humanity. In the resurrection, Christ rolled back the stone of the tomb, but he wants also to break down all the walls that keep us locked in our sterile pessimism, in our carefully constructed ivory towers that isolate us from life, in our compulsive need for security and in boundless ambition that can make us compromise the dignity of others.

When the high priest and the religious leaders, in collusion with the Romans, believed that they could calculate everything, that the final word had been spoken and that it was up to them to apply it, God suddenly breaks in, upsets all the rules, and offers new possibilities. God once more comes to meet us, to create and consolidate a new age, the age of mercy. This is the promise present from the beginning. This is God's surprise for his faithful people. Rejoice! Hidden within your life is a seed of resurrection, an offer of life ready to be awakened.

That is what this night calls us to proclaim: the heartbeat of the risen Lord. Christ is alive! That is what quickened the pace of Mary Magdalene and the other Mary. That is what made them return in haste to tell the news (Matt 28:8). That is what made them lay aside their mournful gait and sad looks. They returned to the city to meet up with the others.

Now that, like the two women, we have visited the tomb, I ask you to go back with them to the city. Let us all retrace our steps and change the look on our faces. Let us go back with them to tell the news . . . In all those places where the grave seems to have the final word, where death seems the only way out. Let us go back to proclaim, to share, to reveal that it is true: the Lord is alive! He is living and he wants to rise again in all those faces that have buried hope, buried dreams, buried dignity. If we cannot let the Spirit lead us on this road, then we are not Christians.

Let us go, then. Let us allow ourselves to be surprised by this new dawn and by the newness that Christ alone can give. May we allow his tenderness and his love to guide our steps. May we allow the beating of his heart to quicken our faintness of heart.

"To Contemplate the Empty Tomb"

Homily for the Easter Vigil

ST. PETER'S BASILICA, THE VATICAN

MARCH 31, 2018

We began this celebration outside, plunged in the darkness of the night and the cold. We felt an oppressive silence at the death of the Lord, a silence with which each of us can identify, a silence that penetrates to the depths of the heart of every disciple, who stands wordless before the cross.

These are the hours when the disciple stands speechless in pain at the death of Jesus. What words can be spoken at such a moment? The disciple keeps silent in the awareness of his or her own reactions during those crucial hours in the Lord's life. Before the injustice that condemned the Master, his disciples were silent. Before the calumnies and the false testimony that the Master endured, his disciples said nothing. During the trying, painful hours of the passion, his disciples dramatically experienced their inability to put their lives on the line to speak out on behalf of the Master. What is more, not only did they not acknowledge him: they hid, they escaped, they kept silent (cf. John 18:25-27).

It is the silent night of the disciples who remained numb, paralyzed, and uncertain of what to do amid so many painful and disheartening situations. It is also that of today's disciples, speechless in the face of situations we cannot control, that make us feel and, even worse, believe that nothing can be done to reverse all the injustices that our brothers and sisters are experiencing in their flesh.

It is the silent night of those disciples who are disoriented because they are plunged in a crushing routine that robs memory, silences hope, and leads to thinking that "this is the way things have always been done." Those disciples who, overwhelmed, have nothing to say and end up considering "normal" and unexceptional the words of Caiaphas: "Can you not see that it is better for you to have one man die for the people than to have the whole nation destroyed?" (John 11:50).

Amid our silence, our overpowering silence, the stones begin to cry out (cf. Luke 19:40) and to clear the way for the greatest message that history has ever heard: "He is not here, for he has been raised" (Matt 28:6). The stone before the tomb cried out and proclaimed the opening of a new way for all. Creation itself was the first to echo the triumph of life over all that had attempted to silence and stifle the joy of the Gospel. The stone before the tomb was the first to leap up and in its own way intone a song of praise and wonder, of joy and hope, in which all of us are invited to join.

Yesterday, we joined the women in contemplating "the one who was pierced" (cf. John 19:36; cf. Zech 12:10). Today, with them, we are invited to contemplate the empty tomb and to hear the words of the angel: "Do not be afraid . . . for he has been raised" (Matt 28:5-6). Those words should affect our deepest convictions and certainties, the ways we judge and deal with the events of our daily lives, especially the ways we relate to others. The empty tomb should challenge us and rally our spirits. It should make us think, but above all it should encourage us to trust and believe that God "happens" in every situation and every person, and that his light can shine in the least expected and most hidden corners of our lives. He rose from the dead, from that place where nobody waits for anything, and now he waits for us—as he did the women—to enable us to share in his saving work. On this basis and with this strength, we Christians place our lives and our energy, our intelligence, our affections, and our will at the service of discovering, and above all creating, paths of dignity.

He is not here . . . he is risen! This is the message that sustains our hope and turns it into concrete gestures of charity. How greatly we need to let our frailty be anointed by this experience! How greatly we need to let our faith be revived! How greatly we need our myopic horizons to be challenged and renewed by this message! Christ is risen, and with him he makes our hope and creativity rise, so that we can face our present problems in the knowledge that we are not alone.

To celebrate Easter is to believe once more that God constantly breaks into our personal histories, challenging our "conventions," those fixed ways of thinking and acting that end up paralyzing us. To celebrate Easter is to allow Jesus to triumph over the craven fear that so often assails us and tries to bury every kind of hope.

The stone before the tomb shared in this, the women of the Gospel shared in this, and now the invitation is addressed once more to you and to me. An invitation to break out of our routines and to renew our lives, our decisions, and our existence. An invitation that must be directed to where we stand, what we are doing, and what we are, with the "power ratio" that is ours. Do we want to share in this message of life or do we prefer simply to continue standing speechless before events as they happen?

He is not here . . . he is raised! And he awaits you in Galilee. He invites you to go back to the time and place of your first love and he says to you: Do not be afraid, follow me. ⌐